What's that smell?

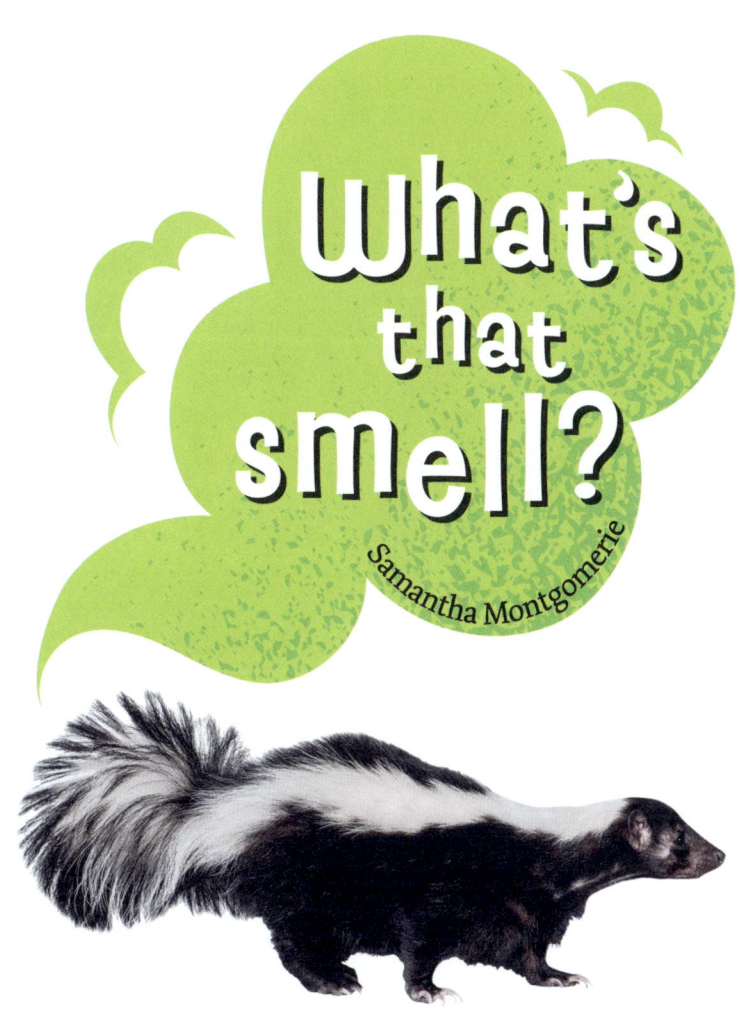

What's that smell?

Samantha Montgomerie

Collins

Contents

Chapter 1 Welcome to our whiffy world! . . 2

What a whiffy world!. 14

Chapter 2 Animal aromas 16

Ring-tailed lemurs: facts 26

Chapter 3 Stinky seas. 28

Spot the spout 40

Chapter 4 Super sniffers 42

How we smell 54

Close-up of a super sniffer 56

Chapter 5 Plants that pong. 58

Meat-eating plants. 70

Chapter 6 Smelly space 72

Stinky Hall of Fame 82

Glossary 84

About the author 86

Book chat 88

CHAPTER 1
Welcome to our whiffy world!

If you are travelling around the globe, there are places where you might want to take a nose plug. Some places on Earth are super-smelly, either because of the natural landscape, or because of the animals who live there.

SMELLY SNIPPET

Humans can smell at least one trillion different scents. We have 400 different odour receptors in our noses.

Smelly residents

Seal Island is a small rocky island near Cape Town in South Africa. It gets it name from its 60,000 resident Cape fur seals and they give their home its special smell! They eat smelly fish, and poo on the rocks where they lie. The stench of thousands of seals in one place is overpowering!

Sometimes humans are responsible for starting a stink. There are some jobs which create extremely strong smells! For example, a large amount of leather is tanned in the city of Fez, in Morocco. Tanning means turning stiff animal skins into soft leather. It's then easy to turn the leather into other things, such as shoes and bags.

The animal skins are smelly when they arrive, so workers wash them in water. Next, the skins go into a smelly bath of cow urine and pigeon droppings.

The leather soaks for hours in this smelly liquid. A chemical called ammonia in the poo and urine helps soften leather. Ammonia has such a strong smell that it makes it hard to breathe! The ancient tanning pits in Fez are outside, so the smell wafts across the city.

Once tanned, the leather is dyed different colours.

FACT!
Some tanning pits in Fez are almost 1,000 years old.

When you drive into the small town of Gilroy in California, US, a garlicky smell will hit your nostrils. This town is known as the Garlic Capital of the World. The largest garlic farm in the United States is there. Every year, they hold a Garlic Festival.

FACT!
Garlic ice cream is a specialty in Gilroy.

Garlic is a little vegetable with a big smell. It has a sulphur **compound** which makes it linger in our bodies when we eat it. If you eat lots, garlic can make your breath, sweat and pee smell.

SMELLY SNIPPET

Sulphur is a chemical which creates a strong smell when it reacts with other things.

Stinky landscapes

When you drive into Rotorua, New Zealand, it smells like rotten eggs! This is because there are lots of hot springs and geysers. The hot water bubbles up from underground and it has lots of smelly sulphur in it. We call this "geothermal activity".

a geothermal lake, Rotorua

FACT!
Geothermal means "heat within the earth". It comes from the Greek words *geo* (earth) and *therme* (heat).

The Pōhutu Geyser in Rotorua is spectacular – it can erupt to a height of 30 metres, spurting hot spring water up into the sky up to 20 times a day. The eggy smell of the heated water fills the air!

SMELLY SNIPPET

The sulphur smell can stay on your clothes and hair, even after you wash them.

There are also bubbling mud pools in Rotorua.

Iceland is another country filled with smelly hot springs. The chemicals left behind from the hot bubbling water and steam make the soil bright yellow and red. This is because of the iron and sulphur in the earth. Many people like to walk through the area and enjoy the scenery – and its eggy smell.

a geothermal valley in Iceland

Iceland is called the "Land of Fire and Ice" because of its mixture of hot springs and icy mountains and glaciers. Underground volcanoes heat up the water for the hot springs found throughout Iceland. The natural spring water can reach temperatures of up to 44 degrees Celsius – that's warmer than a hot bath!

bathing in an Icelandic thermal spring

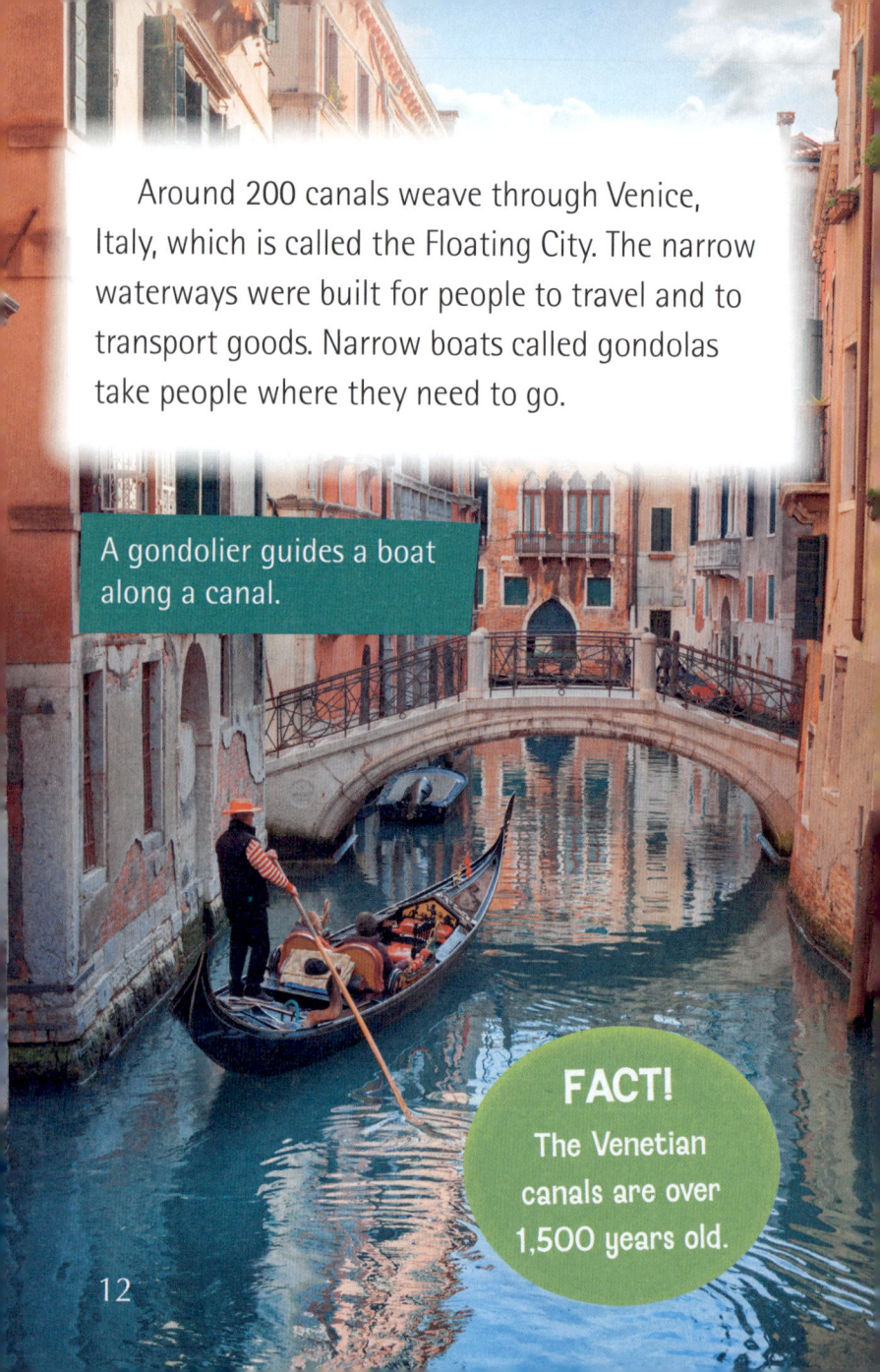

Around 200 canals weave through Venice, Italy, which is called the Floating City. The narrow waterways were built for people to travel and to transport goods. Narrow boats called gondolas take people where they need to go.

A gondolier guides a boat along a canal.

FACT!
The Venetian canals are over 1,500 years old.

Venice has a unique smell. These canals are a mix of freshwater and saltwater, so the city smells like the sea. The tides also play a role in the scents of the city. At low tide, the water level goes down. You can see – and smell – the mud in the canals. It smells pungent, like salty mud and seaweed.

FACT!
Venice is built on 118 small islands separated by the canals.

Grand Canal, Venice

BONUS

What a whiffy world!

Gilroy, US

Cape Town, South Africa

Fludir, Iceland

Venice, Italy

Fez, Morocco

Rotorua, New Zealand

CHAPTER 2
Animal aromas

It's tough surviving in the wild. Many animals use powerful pongs to help them thrive. The animal kingdom is full of stinkers! Some of the smelliest creatures on Earth use their stench to defend themselves, to mark their territory or to attract a partner.

Protective pongs

A stinky scent can be a great way to tell a **predator** to stay away. Many animals use a strong smell to protect themselves.

If you are unlucky enough to be sprayed by a skunk, everyone will know! The smell is like rotten eggs and garlic! It's so strong that it can't be washed off in a shower and it takes days to wear off.

Skunks are slow-moving creatures that are faced with quick predators. If they are going to survive being chased by a fox or coyote, they need a good protection system.

Skunks' short legs make it difficult for them to run fast, but in a flash, they can spin around and lift their tail high. If predators ignore this warning sign, skunks will shower them with their stinky spray, called musk. They can shoot their spray 4.5 metres. Skunks will aim for the predator's face. This causes predators to become temporarily blind, allowing skunks to race away.

Skunks have two special pouches under their tails called **glands**. This is where they store the smelly oil. They can spray five to six times before the glands are empty. It takes six to eight days for the glands to refill, which is the same amount of time that the smell lasts. Skunk musk can be smelt from more than 1.5 kilometres away! This keeps predators away.

SMELLY SNIPPET
The striped skunk's scientific name is *mephitis mephitis*. This comes from the Latin word for "bad odour".

This skunk is getting ready to spray.

Zorillas use a foul-smelling oil to get rid of predators in the same way that skunks do. The stink clings to the zorillas' fur for a long time, which helps when they want to play dead. Predators who come to eat zorillas will take one whiff and steer clear, just in case they eat something that will make them sick.

SMELLY SNIPPET
Even vultures, who eat dead and decaying animal flesh, are reluctant to eat zorillas.

Stay away!

Animals also use strong smells to protect their territory. Marking out their space tells other animals that this area is taken and to keep away. Wolverines spray bushes and trees with a strong musk from glands near their bottom. This musk warns other animals to stay away. They use the same method to coat their food. As you can imagine, this works to stop other animals from stealing it. Would you want to eat food covered in stinky wolverine spray?

FACT!
Wolverines are sometimes called "skunk bears".

Poo makes the perfect smelly signpost to mark out an animal's territory and keep other animals away. Wombat poo is hard and shaped like a cube. This makes it easy for wombats to build a stack of poo so that it doesn't roll away. The smell spreads on the wind and tells other animals to stay away.

wombat poo

Hippopotamuses flick their tails wildly as they poo. This spreads their poo far and wide to mark out their space.

Attractive pongs

Finding the perfect partner in the animal world can be difficult. There is a lot of competition and you have to prove you are the best. Many animals will send out a stench to make sure they are noticed. Musk oxen get their name from the strong smell they give off to attract a mate.

SMELLY SNIPPET
Musk is a strong-smelling substance from the glands of some animals.

Musk oxen have a double coat – a short, fine undercoat and a long top layer. This top layer is the longest fur of any mammal in the world. It can grow 62 centimetres long!

During the breeding season, the male musk oxen's glands produce an oil, which they pee onto their long fur so that it smells strong. Female musk oxen are attracted to the smell and come towards it.

A stink fight is another way to attract a partner in the animal world. Male ring-tailed lemurs have special scent glands in their wrists and shoulders. They will often compete to attract females using scent. Lemurs will rub their tail on their wrists and then wave it in the air to distribute the smell. They use this as a dare for other ringtails to try to "out stink" them.

BONUS

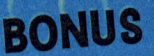

Ring-tailed lemurs: facts

- Their tails are longer than their bodies.
- They live in groups called a "troop".
- Lemurs huddle together to form a "lemur ball" to keep warm and to feel connected.

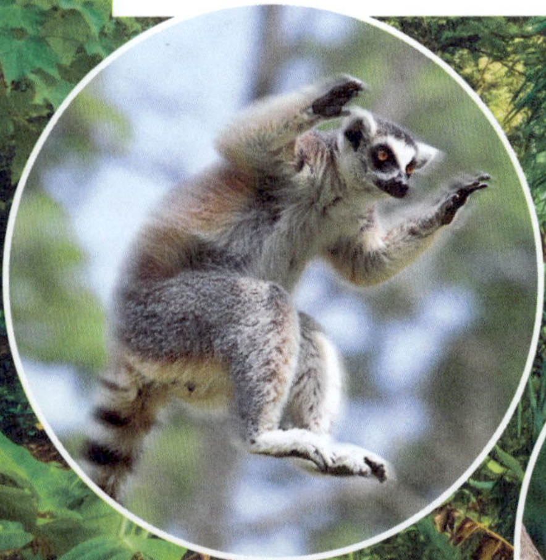

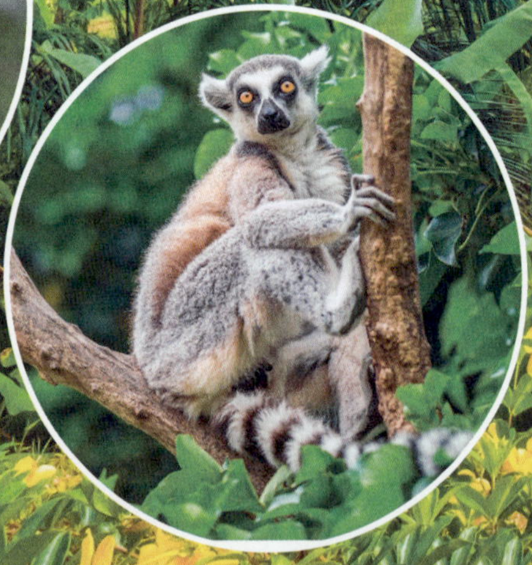

- Their latin name is *catta*, which is the root of the word "cat", because they look a bit like a cat and they purr.

- Ring-tailed lemurs can jump up to a height of three metres.

CHAPTER 3
Stinky seas

Most of us love the smell of the salty sea air, but be warned. Some potent pongs can also linger on the ocean breeze.

The worst breath in the ocean

If you see a humpback whale coming up for breath, hold your nose! These giants have smelly breath, and they are not afraid to let it all out.

a humpback whale spouting

Humpback whales have two blowholes at the top of their heads. These work like our nostrils do, letting the whales breathe air in and out. When they let out their breath, it can travel at incredible speeds, high into the air, creating a spray. This is called a spout. Spouting helps to clear out the whale's blowholes.

a humpback whale's blowhole

Humpback whales are filter feeders. Instead of teeth, they have a filter made of a substance called baleen in their mouths. The baleen makes a sort of net. This strains tiny shrimp-like creatures called krill out of the water. The whale's large mouth swallows the krill whole, and the krill end up in the whale's stomach. The krill rot in there, and that's why humpback whales' spouts stink of rotting fish!

Baleen is made of hard bristles.

A stinky treasure

A rare treasure called ambergris floats in the ocean. It's hard to believe that this stuff, also known as "floating gold", is actually smelly lumps of whale poo.

Ambergris is valuable because of its unusual musky smell. It is used in perfumes and helps to make the scent last longer. People have been using it for over 1,000 years. Today, it costs thousands of pounds per kilogram – making it the most valuable poo in the world!

ambergris

Ambergris comes from sperm whales, that eat a lot of squid. The squid have very hard beaks which are difficult to digest, so the beaks sit inside the whales' stomachs for many years.

a sperm whale

FACT!
Eggs with ambergris was a favourite food of King Charles II of England.

Over time, a waxy substance forms around the squid beaks. It builds up into a tough lump of ambergris. Eventually, the whale poos out the lump. The ambergris is very smelly at first, but after a long time floating in the ocean, it develops a gentler odour. Its musk scent is described as woody and earthy.

A smelly home

Kelp is a giant type of seaweed. There are lots of different sorts of kelp around the globe. During storms, kelp can wash up on beaches. Then it starts to rot and smell. The stench packs a powerful punch, but the smell attracts some creatures who want to make their homes in kelp.

As the kelp begins to rot, **bacteria** inside it give off a strong rotting scent. This is a bit like rotting fruit. Tiny kelp flies pick up on this smell and flock to the kelp. These flies need a constant supply of kelp to eat and lay their eggs on.

a kelp fly

a giant kelp forest

Stinky and inky

Sea hares are slow moving slugs. They don't have a tough shell to protect them, so they're an easy target for predators. These clever creatures have found a smart way of getting out of danger.

FACT!

Sea hares get their name from the pointy bits at the top of their heads, which look like the ears of a hare.

Lobsters like to eat sea hares. When attacked, sea hares protect themselves by producing a cloud of sweet-smelling ink. The lobster thinks this is food and drops the sea hare to eat the ink instead. A chemical in the ink temporarily blocks the predator's nose, stopping its sense of smell. This gives the sea hare enough time to move out of danger.

Sensing scent

Creatures living in the ocean have unique ways of detecting scents to help them survive in their watery world.

A nose for the hunt

Great white sharks are powerful hunters. They have super-sensitive nostrils that help them find their **prey**. These can detect a drop of blood floating in ten billion drops of water! This makes it easy for them to sniff out a potential meal.

Arms that can smell

Octopuses have more than 2,000 scent detectors. Each sucker on their **tentacles** has special cells which can pick up scents. As octopuses explore with their tentacles, they are also sniffing out their next meal.

Feeling the scent

Lobsters use their long antennae to detect smells. When lobsters wave their antennae in the water, the small hairs on the antennae sense smells.

antennae

BONUS

Spot the spout

North Atlantic right whale: V-shaped, up to five metres high

Humpback whale: balloon-shaped, up to three metres high

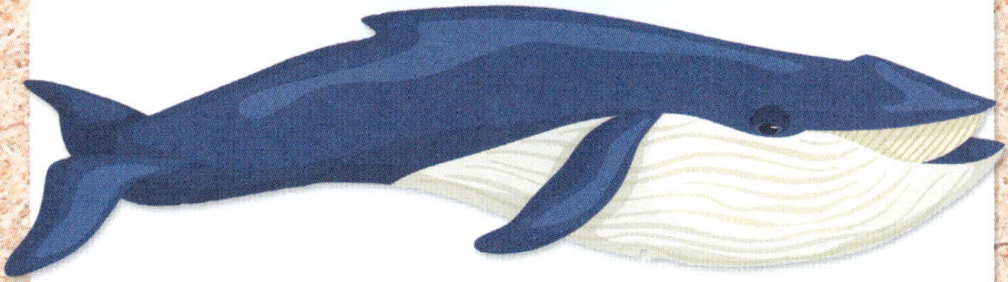

Blue whale: column-shaped, up to six metres high

Sperm whale: slanted, up to three metres high

CHAPTER 4

Super sniffers

Lots of important jobs require a keen sense of smell, from finding missing people to making sure astronauts are safe in space.

Noses at NASA

You don't want to take any chances when you are exploring space. As astronauts prepare to blast off, everything they take with them is thoroughly checked at NASA. This involves a special odour panel.

FACT!
NASA is the US space exploration agency.

When we have an unpleasant smell at home, we can open a window to let in air. You can't do this in space! Odours from things taken to the space station can linger for years, so odour analysts carefully check the smells they are sending into space. A panel of people are chosen to do this important job.

Apollo flight crew

Astronauts must be able to concentrate and not be bothered by unpleasant odours.

Unfamiliar odours may also reduce astronauts' ability to detect important ones, such as a gas leak or something burning. This could be very dangerous.

The odour panel will smell everything heading into space, including books, hats, glues and specialised space equipment.

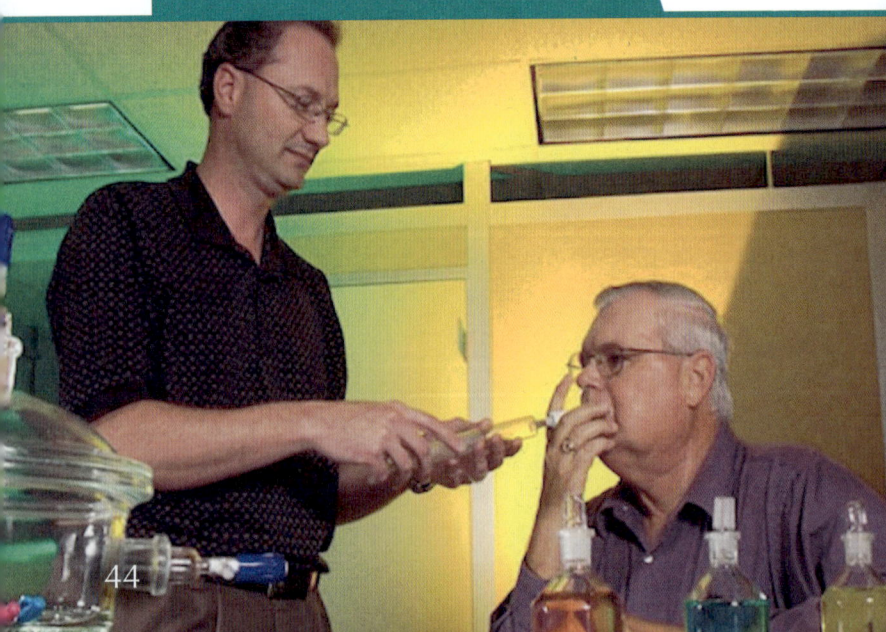

NASA's odour panel testing smells

Taste and smell teamwork

Only about a quarter of what we taste comes from our taste buds. The smell of our food is even more important. Flavour in our food comes from a combination of what we smell and what we taste on our tongue.

FACT!
There are around 10,000 taste-detecting buds on your tongue. They detect five basic tastes – sweet, sour, salty, savoury and bitter.

The happiness of chocolate

Scientists have proven that even a whiff of chocolate can make us feel good! When we smell chocolate, our brains release "feel good" chemicals called endorphins. Endorphins help us let go of stress and feel happy. For this reason, chocolate makers ensure that their chocolate smells just as good as it tastes.

FACT!
The first chocolate was made thousands of years ago in Mexico by the Olmecs.

Some people have the job of chocolate taste tester! They check that chocolate tastes as good as possible, before it is sold. They spend time taking in the scent of the chocolate, noting its particular aromas, before they taste it.

Pooch power

Have you noticed how a dog will thoroughly smell everything around them? This is how they collect information about their world. A dog's sense of smell is their strongest sense. The lining of their nose is much larger than ours, with over 200 million special smell-detecting cells in their nose. This makes them expert sniffers.

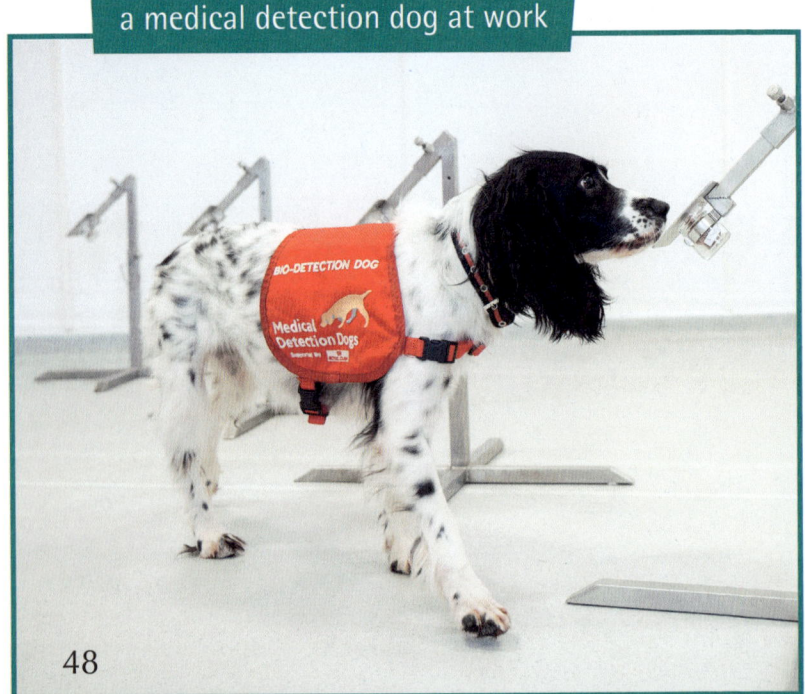

a medical detection dog at work

Dogs detect countless smells that humans can't smell. Search dogs are trained to use this super sense of smell to search for people and save them. If someone is lost, search dogs will use the scent on the person's clothing to find them. They train for six months to two years to become skilled in their work.

Dog brains have 40 times more areas devoted to smell than human brains have.

If someone is buried in an **avalanche**, search dogs use their noses to find them fast. A trained dog can detect the scent of a human through snow as deep as four metres.

Playing tug-of-war with clothing is part of their training. This trains the dogs to pull hard on people's clothing when rescuing them.

Perfume perfection

Since ancient times, people have been combining the scents from flowers, fruits and herbs to make their surroundings smell better. Perfumes are often used directly on the skin, as well as being added to soaps, deodorants and make up.

SMELLY SNIPPET

Ancient Egyptians learnt how to get the scent from flower petals. They would burn the scented oils from the petals in their temples, palaces and homes.

A perfumer's nose knows! These scent artists know exactly what combination of different smells combine to make the perfect perfume. They assemble all the ingredients and train their noses to detect the different aromas. They must get very good at identifying the different mix of smells in a perfume.

SMELLY SNIPPET
A perfumer is sometimes called a "nose"!

Some original ingredients in perfumes may surprise you! Beavers mark their territory with a gooey substance called castoreum which comes from their bottom. This smells like vanilla and was used in perfumes. Perfumers also used musk from deers' glands, which smells like wood and earth. In recent times, **artificial** smells are made to mimic these scents in perfumes. Thankfully, perfumers know how to blend these smells to make them smell amazing!

beaver

BONUS

How we smell

The human olfactory system

Step 1. Sniff: Our nose inhales the smell.

FACT!
Olfactory means relating to the sense of smell.

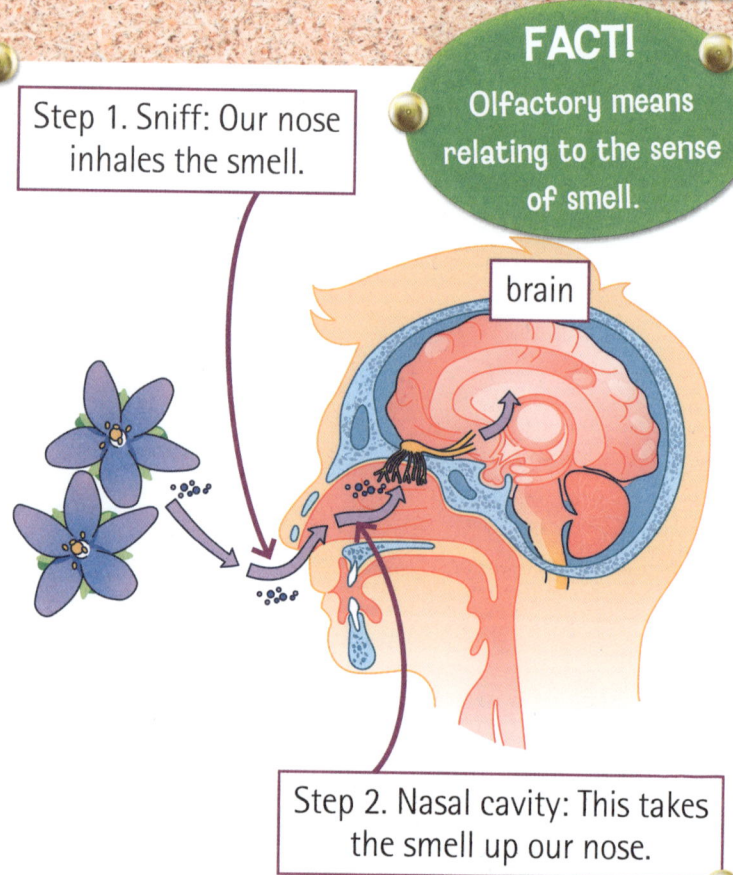

brain

Step 2. Nasal cavity: This takes the smell up our nose.

Step 3. Receptors: These send the smell to our brain.

Step 4. Olfactory bulb: This tells us what we are smelling.

BONUS

Close-up of a super sniffer

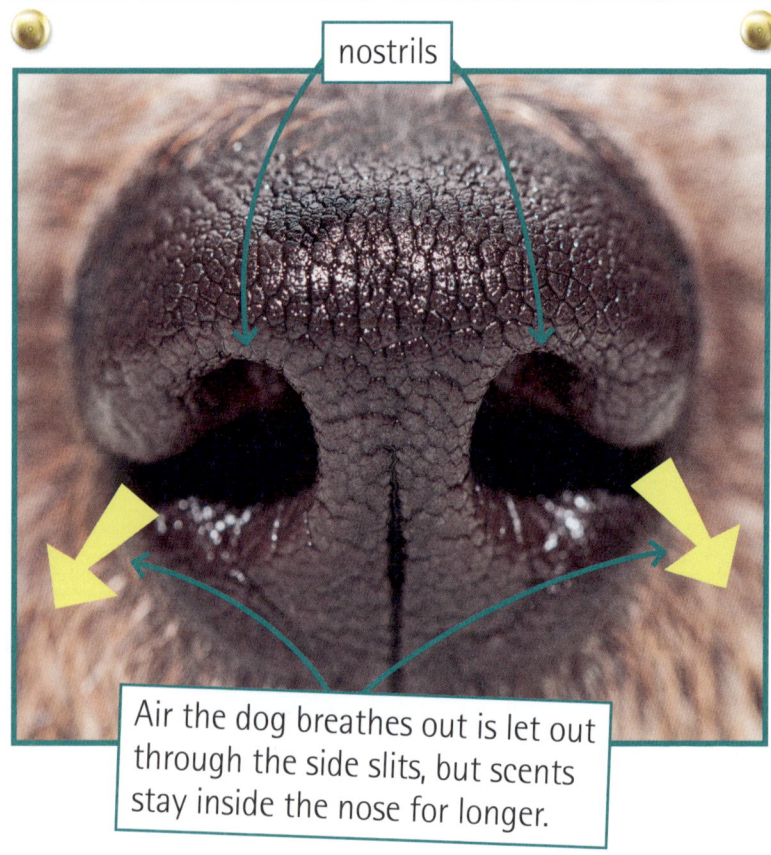

nostrils

Air the dog breathes out is let out through the side slits, but scents stay inside the nose for longer.

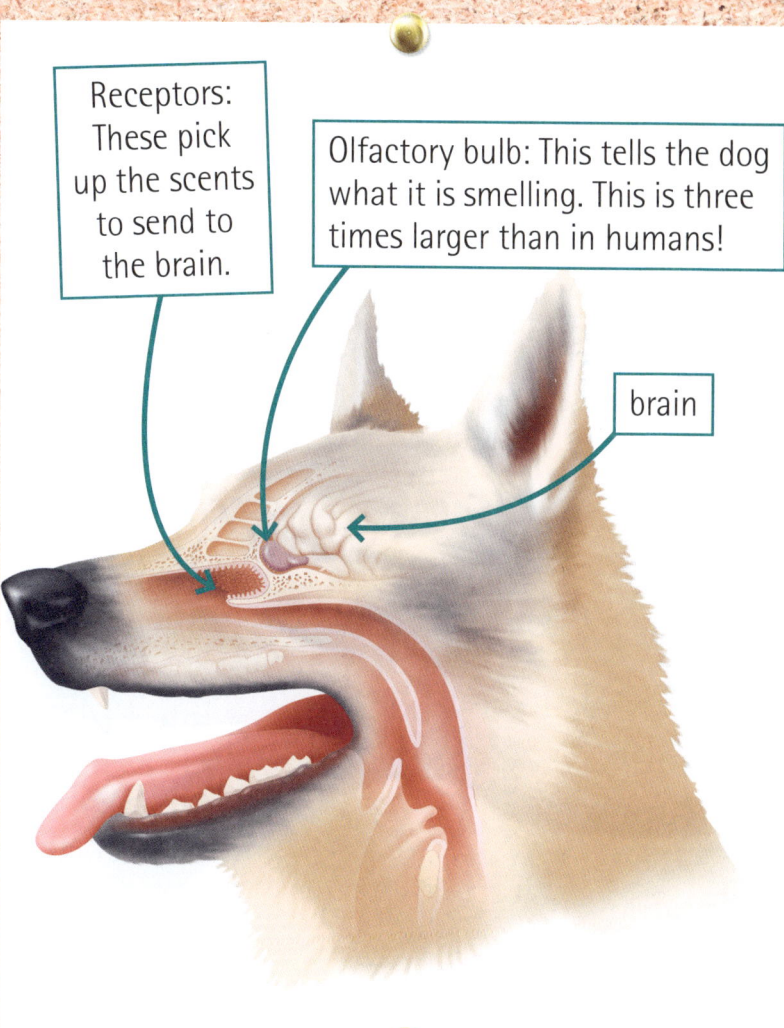

Receptors: These pick up the scents to send to the brain.

Olfactory bulb: This tells the dog what it is smelling. This is three times larger than in humans!

brain

CHAPTER 5
Plants that pong

Hold your nose! Not all flowers are pleasant for us to sniff. Some plants use foul pongs to keep themselves alive.

Pongs for pollinators

Corpse flowers are so dramatic. They take ten years to flower, tower into the air and smell like rotting flesh. Corpse flowers are officially called *titan arums*, but they get their nickname because they smell like something that has died!

Corpse flowers make a tall spear which grows up to three metres high. The sheer size of these plants is unusual. Scientists believe the flowers grow this big to look like a large decaying animal. Along with their smell, this attracts **scavengers**, such as beetles and flies. They think the plant is a rotting animal – their favourite food.

When the insects land on the plant, the pollen sticks to their bodies. They quickly discover that it's not good to eat, and fly off, taking pollen with them. When they go to other plants, they spread this pollen to the other plants which can then make seeds.

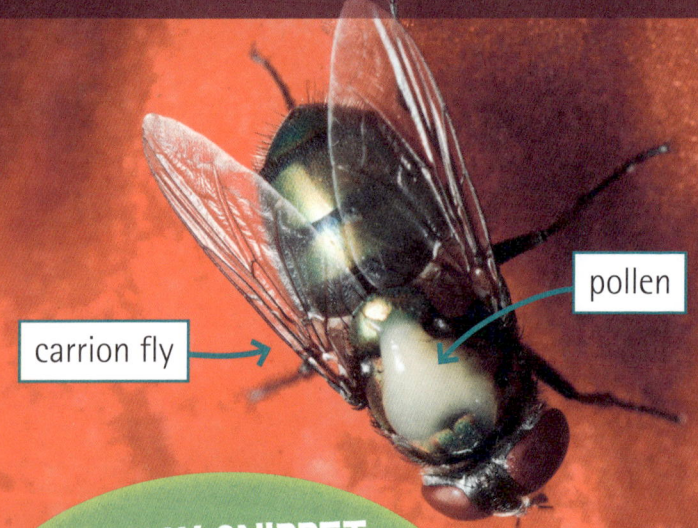

carrion fly

pollen

SMELLY SNIPPET

There are corpse flowers in public gardens around the world. Lots of people visit the gardens to see – and smell – this extraordinary plant.

Stinking corpse lilies attract pollinators in a similar way to the corpse flower. As well as smelling putrid, the red petals are the colour of blood and have a tough and warty surface. The flower appears to have fur, whiskers and teeth, which make it look even more like a dead animal.

the warty surface and tooth-like inside of the corpse lily

Stink to survive

Plants need to spread their seeds in order to reproduce and form new plants. Some plants use smells to attract animals, who can carry their seeds to other places.

The grey-headed flying-fox uses its keen sense of smell to locate figs.

Many plants produce a tasty package to keep their seeds in, such as fruit. This protects the seeds as they grow. When the seeds inside the plant are ready, the plant drops the fruit. The smell of the fruit will attract an animal to it. The animal will eat the fruit, seeds and all.

A blackbird eats a rowan berry filled with seeds.

FACT!
Seeds can be carried by air, water or animals.

After eating the fruit, the animal moves on. Land animals, such as deer, cover short distances while birds can fly great distances from where they ate the food. When the animals poo out the seeds, the seeds fall to the ground and start to grow. Apples, pears and berries all distribute their seeds in this way.

The scent of a ripe apple attracts animals to eat the fruit – and the seeds inside.

With a crown of golden leaves, gingko trees are beautiful. However, in late autumn, female gingko trees start to smell rotten. They produce a fruit with a chemical inside. This is the same chemical that makes vomit smell so bad.

gingko tree

ripe ginyko fruit

Gingko trees date back 200 million years – it's one of the only living tree species that existed with dinosaurs! They are so ancient that we are not sure what animals would have eaten its fruit. Animals today won't touch it until the smelly casing has rotted away and the seeds are left.

FACT!
Gingko trees have been around so long, they are known as "living **fossils**"!

A flower that smells like a sweaty fox would keep most people away! Crown imperial flowers smell like a mix of wet fox fur and garlic. This has earned it the nickname of "sweaty fox flower". Its smell keeps animals such as mice and rabbits away, protecting it from being eaten.

SMELLY SNIPPET

Gardeners plant the sweaty fox flower to put animals off coming into the garden, protecting their plants from being eaten.

Treat traps

Some plants use smells to attract food to them! Pitcher plants are **carnivorous**. They produce a sweet-smelling nectar on the rim of their leaf to tempt their prey. Animals such as spiders, frogs or mice will be attracted to the scent, thinking it is food.

Pitcher plants have a slippery wax on their leaves causing animals to slip inside. They fall into a pool of liquid inside the leaves. The more animals struggle to get out, the more they sink. The liquid **dissolves** the animals so that the plants can eat them. The plants then absorb the animals until all that's left is fur and bone.

A pitcher is a big jug. The pitcher plant gets its name due to its shape.

BONUS

Meat-eating plants

Meat-eating plants have different methods to trap their prey.

1. The pitfall: a slippery patch makes prey fall into the plant

pitcher plant

2. Snapping traps: small hairs trigger the plant to snap closed around the prey

Venus fly trap

3. Sucking traps: underwater pouches open and suck prey inside

bladderwort

4. Sticky traps: prey get stuck on the plant

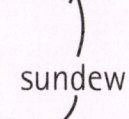

sundew

CHAPTER 6
Smelly space

You might think that there wouldn't be much to smell in the emptiness of space. But actually, astronauts and scientists have discovered that there are lots of pungent smells out there! The planets and moons of our solar system are made of lots of different gases and chemicals, and many of these are smelly.

FACT!
The solar system is the Sun and everything that travels around the Sun.

It isn't safe for astronauts to take off their helmets to see what space smells like. No astronaut has actually been able to take off their helmet to take a sniff. However, when astronauts return from a spacewalk, they are able to detect scents from their explorations outside.

Astronauts have detected odours clinging to their helmets, suits and gloves. These scents help us to learn more about space. Many have returned from a spacewalk and reported a smell on their suits like burning metal.

an astronaut on a spacewalk

Gunpowder moon

All of the astronauts who have set foot on the moon agree on one thing – the moon smells like fireworks. When returning from their moonwalks, a fine dust remains on their spacesuits. A smell like ashes or an explosion comes from this dust.

Scientists are exploring what gives moon dust this smell. They have found there are no smelly **molecules** in the dust itself. They think that the smell must come from a chemical reaction when the astronauts enter back into the spacecraft. Petrichor is the name of the earthy smell that soil makes when it rains. Moondust reacting with water could have a similar effect.

> The moon's surface is covered in fine dust from **meteorites** crashing into it.

Comet stench

When scientists landed a spacecraft on a comet for the first time, they were surprised to find a serious stink there. The spacecraft Rosetta was able to land on a comet named 67P. It detected chemicals in the comet that smell of rotten eggs, vinegar, cat pee and bitter almonds.

The tail of a comet is called a coma. It forms as the energy from the Sun pushes some of the comet's dust and gases into long streams. The Rosetta spacecraft found that as the tail formed on comet 67P, the comet started to give off the whiffy chemicals.

coma   nucleus

A giant stink

Far away from the Sun, in the cold outer reaches of our solar system, sit four giant planets – Saturn, Uranus, Jupiter and Neptune. These planets have no solid surface and are huge globes of gas and liquid. They would make a stinky stench if we could smell them! This is due to the gases they are made from.

FACT!
Scientists call the outer planets "gas giants", though they consist mostly of liquid and have solid cores.

Jupiter

Mighty Jupiter is the largest planet in our solar system. It is more than twice as large as all the other planets put together. Jupiter is made up of a number of gases, and some are very stinky. Ammonia, hydrogen sulphide and phosphine are three stinky chemicals in its gases. If we could take a sniff, Jupiter would probably smell like sweat, urine and rotten eggs!

FACT!
Jupiter is named after the king of the Roman gods.

Unless you like pinching your nose, it's a good thing you don't live on Uranus! Scientists used a tool called a spectrometer to examine what was in the blue-green clouds of Uranus. They found evidence of the chemical hydrogen sulphide in the gas around Uranus. This makes a whiffy rotten egg smell.

Uranus

FACT!
Uranus has a large tilt which makes it spin on its side.

Raspberry cloud

Our home galaxy is called the Milky Way. Rather than tasting like milk, the Milky Way may taste like sweet raspberries. At the centre of our galaxy there is a vast dust cloud. Within this cloud is a substance called ethyl formate. This is what gives some fruits their sweet smell and it tastes a little like raspberries.

the Milky Way

Our solar system

Our solar system includes the Sun and everything that **orbits** the Sun. It is a small part of a vast system of stars in the Milky Way galaxy. The Milky Way is one of billions of galaxies in the universe. One day, we might be able to explore other incredible smells outside of our galaxy!

Sun

Venus

Mars

Mercury

Earth

Jupiter

FACT!

Our solar system is ancient. Scientists believe it is roughly 4.5 billion years old! It formed from a cloud of gas and dust.

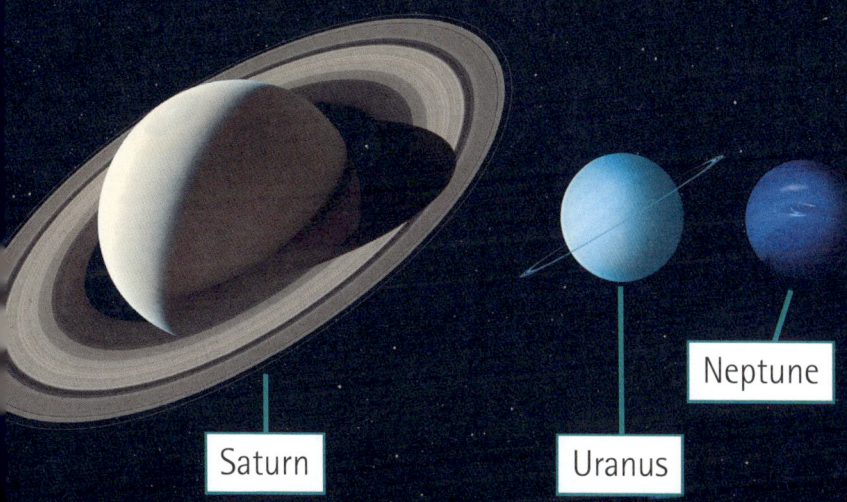

Saturn

Uranus

Neptune

BONUS
Stinky Hall of Fame

Stinkiest Planet

Jupiter

Pongiest Plant

Corpse flowers

Worst Breath in the Ocean

Humpback whales

Smelliest Food Protection Tactic

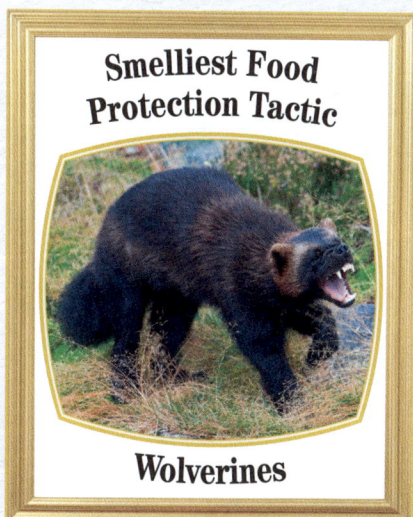

Wolverines

Best Nose

Dogs

Reekiest Residents

Cape fur seals

Glossary

artificial made by humans to seem like something natural

avalanche a large amount of snow that moves quickly down a slope

bacteria tiny living things that can be found in all natural environments

carnivorous eats mostly meat

compound a substance made from two or more different things

dissolves melts or becomes liquid

fossils the remains of prehistoric plants or animals that have hardened into rock

glands organs in an animal's body which produce something important

meteorites rocks that fall from space

molecules groups of atoms which form the smallest unit of a substance

orbits travels around a star or planet

predator an animal that hunts other animals for food

prey animals that are killed and eaten by other animals

receptors cells in different parts of the body that respond to our senses and send signals to our brains

scavengers animals that find and eat dead animals or rotting plants

tentacles long, flexible structures that stick out from the head or mouth of an animal and help it to feel or grasp things

About the author

Why did you want to be an author?

I've always enjoyed reading and learning. I also love to play with words. Writing non-fiction books allows me to do both things! I can find out about new and interesting topics and share them with readers.

Samantha Montgomerie

How did you start writing?

I used to fill pages and pages with stories as a young child, tying them together with wool and spending a long time making colourful covers. I guess that is where the journey as a writer first began. As an adult, when my first book was published, I was so excited! I decided that was what I wanted to do for the rest of my life.

Why did you choose to write this book?

There are some truly awful smells in our world – and usually there is a good reason for the pong! I was interested in why so many things stink and the unusual reasons why they do.

How did you pick which smelly animals to include?

This was difficult – there are so many stinky creatures out there! In the end I chose ones which made the stinkiest stench. I also tried to think about the different ways they used their smells.

What do you hope readers will get from this book?

Our sense of smell is so important for finding out about our world. We can learn so much about how animals behave, how our natural world works, what we know about space, and how our sense of smell helps us to taste and to learn about our world.

What was the most interesting thing you learnt writing this book?

That the Milky Way smells like raspberries!

What smells do you like?

Chocolate, my cat Izzy and the smell of a new book are my favourite smells. Reading a new book while eating chocolate with Izzy on my lap – this combination is perhaps the best smell of all!

Book chat

Have you ever seen any of the animals or plants in the book in real life?

What's the stinkiest thing in nature you've ever smelled?

What's your favourite smell?

What's your least favourite smell?

What was the most surprising thing you learnt in the book?

Which thing in this book would you most like and least like to smell?

How does a sense of smell help us humans?

Can you think of other ways that animals protect themselves, other than smell?

Do you think you'd be a good smell tester at NASA?

What was your favourite chapter in the book?

Do you have a favourite photo in the book?

If you could learn more about one animal, plant or place from this book, which one would you choose and why?

Who would you recommend this book to and why?

If someone asked you to describe this book in one sentence, what would you say?

If you could ask the author one question, what would it be?

If you had to think of a new title for this book, what would you call it?

Book challenge:
Create your own Hall of Fame of favourite smells.

Published by Collins An imprint of HarperCollins*Publishers*

The News Building
1 London Bridge Street
London
SE1 9GF
UK

Macken House
39/40 Mayor Street Upper
Dublin 1
D01 C9W8
Ireland

© HarperCollins*Publishers* Limited 2025

10 9 8 7 6 5 4 3 2 1

ISBN 978-0-00-874641-4

All rights reserved. No part of this publication may be reproduced, stored in a retrieval system, or transmitted in any form by any means, electronic, mechanical, photocopying, recording or otherwise, without the prior written permission of the Publisher or a licence permitting restricted copying in the United Kingdom issued by the Copyright Licensing Agency Ltd, 5th Floor, Shackleton House, 4 Battle Bridge Lane, London SE1 2HX.

Without limiting the author's and publisher's exclusive rights, any unauthorised use of this publication to train generative artificial intelligence (AI) technologies is expressly prohibited. HarperCollins also exercise their rights under Article 4(3) of the Digital Single Market Directive 2019/790 and expressly reserve this publication from the text and data mining exception.

British Library Cataloguing-in-Publication Data
A catalogue record for this publication is available from the British Library.

Download the teaching notes and word cards to accompany this book at:
http://littlewandle.org.uk/signupfluency/

Get the latest Collins Big Cat news at
collins.co.uk/collinsbigcat

Author: Samantha Montgomerie
Publisher: Laura White
Product managers: Caroline Green
　　and Holly Woolnough
Series editor: Charlotte Raby
Development editor: Catherine Baker
Commissioning editor: Caroline Green
Project manager: Emily Hooton
Copyeditor: Sally Byford
Proofreader: Catherine Dakin
Cover designer: Sarah Finan
Typesetter: 2Hoots Publishing Services Ltd
Production controller: Katharine Willard

Printed in the UK.

MIX
Paper | Supporting responsible forestry
FSC™ C007454

This book contains FSC™ certified paper and other controlled sources to ensure responsible forest management.
For more information visit: www.harpercollins.co.uk/green

Made with responsibly sourced paper and vegetable ink

Scan to see how we are reducing our environmental impact.

Acknowledgements
The publishers gratefully acknowledge the permission granted to reproduce the copyright material in this book. Every effort has been made to trace copyright holders and to obtain their permission for the use of copyright material. The publishers will gladly receive any information enabling them to rectify any error or omission at the first opportunity.

Front cover Eric Isselee/Shutterstock, Back cover Eric Isselee/Shutterstock, p20 Hemis/Alamy, p21 & p83tl Arterra Picture Library/Alamy, p34 FLPA/Alamy, p37 imageBROKER.com GmbH & Co. KG / Alamy, p41b Kirk Hewlett/Alamy, pp42–43 The Print Collector/Alamy, p43 Science History Images/Alamy, p44 NASA, p48 Leon Neal/Getty Images, p57 BSIP SA/Alamy, p60 Minden Pictures/Alamy, p71tr Nature Picture Library/Alamy.

All other photos Shutterstock.